Think not those who are slain in the way of Allah as dead.
Nay, they are alive. They are with their Lord being sustained.
Chapter 3 Al-Imran, ayah No 169

Worldwide Publishing and distribution except for U.S.A. & Canada by
Alif Publishing Ltd
email siddiqa@alif.co.uk

Published and Distributed in U.S.A. & Canada by
Khatoons Inc.
6650 Autumn Wind Circle. Clarksville, MD 21029 USA
Phone (410) 531-9653 - email info@khatoons.com - www.khatoons.com

Written and Illustrated by Siddiqa Juma

Dedicated to my Mother and Father

BEFORE KARBALA

A long time ago in Makkah there were two brothers, Abdu-Shams and Hashim. They were direct descendants of Prophet Ibrahim. They were appointed to look after the pilgrims who came to Makkah. When Abdu-Shams died, his adopted son Umayya thought that he would take his father's place, but because Umayya was known to be dishonest, the elders of Makkah decided that he should not take over his father's duties and instead, Hashim should be given the responsibilities. Umayya became angry and started being very rude towards Hashim. When the elders of the tribe saw this, they decided that he should not be allowed to remain in Makkah, and was therefore sent to Syria. This was the beginning of the hatred of the Umayya family towards the Hashimi family which eventually led to the martyrdom of Imam Hussain (a.s.)

There were many different tribes living in Makkah. The tribe which came from Hashim were known as the Banu Hashim, and those from Umayya as the Banu Umayya. Hashim was the great grandfather of Prophet Muhammad (s.a.w.) and

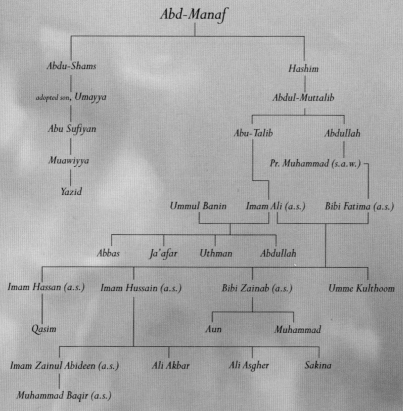

As well as some of the names mentioned above, other members of the Prophet's family also fought in the battle of Karbala

that is why the families of the Prophet are known as the Banu Hashim. Although the Banu Hashim were not as rich as the Banu Umayya, they were always respected more because they were kind and always ready to help others. This made the Banu Umayya very jealous of them. When the Prophet (s.a.w.) started preaching, the people of Makkah gave him so much trouble that he decided to leave his home and go to Madina. In the second year of Hijra, the Prophet's cousin, Imam Ali (a.s.) married the Prophet's only daughter Fatima (a.s.). They had four children, Imam Hassan (a.s.), Imam Hussain (a.s.), Bibi Zainab and Umme Kulthoom. Imam Hussain (a.s.) was born on the 3rd of Sha'baan in the fourth year of Hijra.

The Prophet (s.a.w.) loved all his grand children very much. One day, when he was in Sajdah while praying in the mosque, Imam Hussain (a.s.) climbed on his back. The Prophet remained in Sajdah until Imam Hussain (a.s.) came down himself.

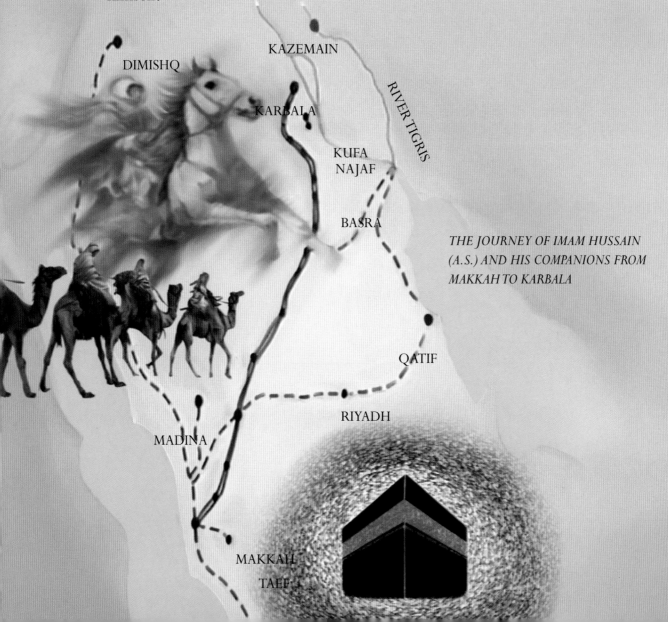

KAZEMAIN

DIMISHQ

RIVER TIGRIS

KARBALA

KUFA
NAJAF

BASRA

THE JOURNEY OF IMAM HUSSAIN (A.S.) AND HIS COMPANIONS FROM MAKKAH TO KARBALA

QATIF

RIYADH

MADINA

MAKKAH
TAEF

Imam Hussain (a.s.) was always ready to defend Islam and fight against the evil leaders like Mu'awiya, governor of Syria and the great grandson of Umayya. Mu'awiya severely punished anybody who spoke against him. He sent his army to fight against Imam Ali (a.s.) at Siffeen in Iraq. They took over the river Euphrates and stopped Imam Ali (a.s.) and his army from getting any water. Imam Hassan and Imam Hussain (a.s.) who were now young men, led a group of fighters and got back the control of the river from the enemy. Imam Ali (a.s.) allowed everyone to use the river including the enemies. It was on this same river 23 years later that Imam Hussain (a.s.) fought his final battle for the sake of saving Islam.

When Imam Ali (a.s.) became the khalifa (leader of the Muslims) at the age of 57, he removed all the governors who were mistreating people. Muawiya refused to give up his post, and continued to fight Imam Ali (a.s.). Muawiya ordered Ibn Muljim to kill Imam Ali (a.s.). On the 19th of Ramadhan in the 40th year of Hijra Ibn Muljim struck Imam Ali (a.s.) with a poison sword while he was praying in a mosque in kufa.

On the 21st month of Ramadhan, Imam Ali (a.s.) died at the age of 63. After the martyrdom of Imam Ali (a.s.), Imam Hassan (a.s.) was chosen by the people of Kufa as their leader. When Imam Hassan (a.s.) saw the situation that the Muslims were facing at that time, he decided that it was in the interest of Islam not to fight Mu'awiya. Imam Hassan (a.s.) entered into an agreement with him, that he would not oppose him as long as he did not make the Muslims suffer. Also, another condition was that after the death of Mu'awiya the people would be allowed to appoint their own leader. Mu'awiya knew that there was no way he was going to succeed in his evil ways as long as Imam Hassan (a.s.) was alive. He promised Imam Hassan's wife, Ju'da, that if she killed her husband, he would pay her one hundred thousand dirhams. He also promised to marry her to his son Yazid and so Ju'da poisoned Imam Hassan (a.s.). Imam Hassan (a.s.) died on the 28th of Safar in the 50th year of Hijra. The people were forced to accept Yazid as their leader after Mu'awiya's death.

KARBALA

Imam Hussain (a.s.) had seen how the people of Kufa had not come to his father's help when he needed them, and how they had mistreated his brother Imam Hassan (a.s.). Still, he considered it as his duty to help anyone who needed him. He immediately asked his cousin Muslim ibn Aqeel to proceed to Kufa, and he was going to follow him later.

When Yazid came to know about what was happening in Kufa, he sent Ibn Ziyad, a well-known enemy of the Prophet's family to Kufa, and ordered him to put all tribal leaders into prisons, and arrest Muslim ibn Aqeel. That evening after prayers, when Muslim ibn Aqeel was walking home alone in the dark alleyways of Kufa, he heard that Ibn Ziyad had offered a reward to anyone who handed him in. Muslim ibn Aqeel ran into an old woman's house and hid there. When her son came to know about it, he reported him. Muslim ibn Aqeel was arrested, and then thrown from the rooftop of the governor's palace. His dead body was dragged in the streets of Kufa for everyone to see.

Imam Hussain (a.s.) received the sad news while he was on his way to Kufa to join Muslim ibn Aqeel. Ibn Ziyad was well prepared for Imam Husain's arrival. Every road leading into Kufa was blocked and guarded by his troops. He sent an army of one thousand men led by Hurr to stop him from entering the city. By the time they met Imam Husain's (a.s.) caravan Hurr and his troops had run out of water and were nearly dying of thirst. When Imam Hussain (a.s.) saw the state they were in, he gave them water even though they were his enemy. Hurr spoke to Imam Hussain (a.s.) about his orders to stop him from entering Kufa. He told him not continue towards Kufa, but to go to Karbala.

Imam Hussain (a.s.) together with his companions reached Karbala on the 2nd of Muharram in the 61st year of Hijra. He set up camp by the banks of the river Euphrates known as the Alqama. The land belonged to the Banu Asad. He told them that soon he and his companions would be killed and their bodies would be left unburied. He requested the Banu Asad to bury them after everyone had left. Imam Hussain (a.s.) bought the land from them and gave it back to them as a gift.

On the 3rd of Muharram ibn Ziyad sent an army led by Umar Saad. His orders were to get Imam Hussain (a.s.) to surrender to Yazid. When Imam Hussain (a.s.) refused, Yazid told ibn Ziyad to send more troops. Ibn Ziyad ordered all the men in Kufa to come out and join the army to fight against Imam Hussain (a.s.). Anyone refusing to do so would be killed.

Meanwhile, Umar Saad ordered Imam Hussain (a.s.) to move away from the water site. Imam Hussain (a.s.) did not resist. They moved their camp several miles away. He did not want the people to think that the battle in Karbala was about water. By the seventh day of Muharram Imam Husain's camp had run out of water. The women and young children in his camp showed great patience as well as courage. The children were especially thirsty in the hot desert sun of Karbala. Hurr remembered how kind Imam Hussain (a.s.) was when he needed water. He asked Umar Saad to give water to Imam Husain's (a.s.) camp or at least to the children, but Umar Saad showed no pity.

On the 9th of Muharram a final warning was sent to Imam Hussain (a.s.) from Umar Saad that if he did not surrender, he would be killed. Imam Hussain (a.s.) refused to bow down to his threats. Imam Hussain (a.s.) and his companions spent that evening praying and reciting Qur'an.

That night Hurr was feeling very guilty, and blamed himself for bringing Imam Hussain (a.s.) to Karbala. He talked to his son and his slave about going to fight on the side of Imam Hussain (a.s.). They agreed with his decision and went with him. When they reached Imam Husain's (a.s.) camp, Hurr with tears in his eyes said "O my Imam I am sorry for forcing you to come to Karbala. Please allow me to fight along with you. I would be honoured if you would let me lay down my life first before anyone amongst you is killed. I have brought my son to die with me defending your sons". Imam Hussain (a.s.) was deeply moved by Hurr's words. He welcomed him saying that he considered him his special guest. Hurr was amazed by his kindness.

It was time for morning prayers. Imam Hussain (a.s.) asked his son Ali Akbar, who looked exactly like his grandfather Muhammad (s.a.w.) to give the 'adhaan'. After the prayers, Imam Hussain (a.s.) went to the enemy camp and explained to them who he was and what was his beliefs. He said that he was a peaceful man wishing to live a peaceful life, and did not wish to harm anybody. By killing him they would be committing a sin against the family of the Prophet (s.a.w.). Imam Hussain (a.s.) made this speech so that later no one would be able to say that it was Imam Hussain (a.s.) who started this battle. Umar Saad became worried that Imam Husain's (a.s.) words might change the minds of some of the troops. He stood up and said in a loud voice, "Everyone in my army bear witness that I am firing the first arrow in this battle." He put an arrow to his bow and shot it towards Imam Husain's (a.s.) tent. There followed thousands of arrows towards Imam Husain's (a.s.) camp.

Back at the camp, Hurr asked Imam Hussain (a.s.) for permission to go and face the enemy. He mounted his horse together with his son and his slave and rode towards the battle field. Hurr faced the enemy and told them that until last night he was with them but he realised just in time that by fighting on Yazid's side he was going to fight against truth and justice. He asked them to think carefully about what they were about to do. Umar Saad realised that if Hurr was allowed to say any more, every thing would be lost. He ordered his army to attack Hurr, his son and his slave. The son and the slave were killed first. Hurr continued bravely until an arrow struck him on his forehead and he fell. Imam Hussain (a.s.) rushed to his side. He took a handkerchief which had belonged to his mother Fatima (a.s.) and tied it on his bleeding wound. He put his hand on Hurr's head and said "May Allah bless you my friend." Hurr died in Imam Hussain's (a.s.) arms.

After Hurr, one by one of Imam Hussain's companions went onto the battlefield and fought bravely against the enemy. On each occasion when one of them fell, Imam Hussain (a.s.), Hazrat Abbas and Ali Akbar would rush out to be by the side of their dying companion. Imam Hussain's (a.s.) companions were determined that as long as one of them was alive, they would not allow the blood of Imam Hussain (a.s.) and his family spill in Karbala. From early that morning, Imam Hussain (a.s.) together with Hazrat Abbas, Ali Akbar and others carried the bodies of their companions back to the camp. Although these brave soldiers did not have their own families to mourn their death, the ladies in Imam Hussain's (a.s.) camp cried for them as if they were part of their own family.

As the sun rose higher in the desert sky, the heat became more intense by the minute. The children were crying for water. Some of the remaining companions approached the river banks to get some water but were stopped by the enemy. They fought bravely and were killed in battle. Sadly, no water reached the thirsty children of Karbala.

It was now midday, and the time for Zuhur prayer was approaching. Imam Hussain (a.s.) led the prayers while three of his companions stood in front of the prayer line to shield the Imam. The enemy fired arrows towards them, and by the time the prayer ended, the companions who were protecting them were dying of arrow wounds. All the companions had now been killed. Only Imam Hussain (a.s.) and a handful of his family were left to fight the huge army of Yazid.

First Ali Akbar asked for his father's permission to go to the battlefield. Imam Hussain (a.s.) looked at his young son lovingly, and said how he reminded him of the Prophet (s.a.w.) in every way. He gave Ali Akbar his blessings, and told him to go to his mother and aunt. Ali Akbar greeted his mother Umme Laila and aunt Bibi Zainab. Umme Laila with tears in her eyes looked at the 18 year old Ali Akbar and said, "O God is it time for you to go ?" With these words she fell into Ali Akbar's arms and fainted.

The battle drums of the enemies were now getting louder and louder. Ali Akbar went to the battlefield, and faced the enemy with all the bravery that he inherited from his grandfather Imam Ali (a.s.). He reminded the enemy that his father, Imam Hussain (a.s.) spent his life in the way of Islam, and did no harm to them. By spilling his blood they were making the Prophet (s.a.w.) very sad. Umar Saad told his troops not to listen to Ali Akbar, and ordered them to attack him. One by one he fought them with great skill, and killed many of them. Ali Akbar received several wounds, and was losing a lot of blood. The thirst was getting more unbearable. At that moment he longed to see his loved ones for the last time.

Ali Akbar turned his horse back towards his camp. He found his father standing at the entrance of the tent, watching the battle between his beloved thirsty son and the enemy. Imam Hussain (a.s.) congratulated his son and then said, "I am sad that I do not have any water to give you." Ali Akbar met each and every one of his family. They were all in tears because they knew that this time he wasn't coming back alive. As Ali Akbar rode towards the battlefield Imam Hussain (a.s.) looked up to the sky and said, "Allah be witness to the fact that I am sending my son who looks like the Prophet (s.a.w.) to be martyred for the sake of truth and justice."

It was not long before Imam Hussain (a.s.) heard the painful cry from the battlefield. Ali Akbar fell with a fatal wound in his chest. He called out to his father to come to him quickly. Imam Hussain (a.s.) went towards his son, and found him lying in a pool of his own blood. When he saw his son he cried out, "Here I am my son, please talk to me." Ali Akbar was in great pain, the broken end of the arrow was sticking out of his chest, and blood was gushing out. Ali Akbar died in his father's arms. Imam Hussain (a.s.) lifted Ali Akbar carefully, as if protecting him from any more pain. He cried all the way back to his camp. When he reached the camp, Umme Laila, Bibi Zainab, Umme Kulthoom, and the other ladies and children all rushed out to see Ali Akbar. When Umme Laila saw how much Imam Hussain (a.s.) was crying, she said, "I am really proud of our son for sacrificing his life for such a noble cause. I pray to Allah that he may grant us patience."

Aun and Muhammad felt that after the martyrdom of their cousin Ali Akbar it was now their turn to go to the battlefield. They went to their mother Bibi Zainab, to ask for her blessings. Aun and Muhammad assured their mother that they would fight with such bravery that whenever she thought of them, she would remember how brave they were. Bibi Zainab went to her brother to request him to let her sons follow in the footsteps of Ali Akbar. Imam Hussain (a.s.) looked at his sister and said, "My beloved sister you have never asked me for anything before, how can I say no to you now." He turned to Aun and Muhammad and said, "Go my sons, be brave. I shall join you soon on your journey to the heavens." Bibi Zainab held them close and kissed them goodbye.

Imam Hussain (a.s.), Hazrat Abbas and Imam Hassan's son Qasim, stood by Bibi Zainab as she watched her sons go off to fight. Hardly a few minutes had passed when Aun fell from his horse and shouted for Imam Hussain (a.s.). Just at that moment another cry was heard, this time from Muhammad. Hazrat Abbas left Qasim with Bibi Zainab and ran to the battlefield. Imam Hussain (a.s.) carried the body of Muhammad while Hazrat Abbas carried Aun. When they reached the camp Bibi Zainab came over to see her sons and thanked Allah for accepting the martyrdom of her sons. Imam Hussain (a.s.), Hazrat Abbas, Qasim and the ladies were all crying by her side.

Qasim told his mother that he would also like to go and fight for his uncle Imam Hussain (a.s.). His mother Umme Farwa said, "My son before your father died he told me that there would come a time when his brother Imam Hussain (a.s.) would be surrounded by blood-thirsty enemies. He would have been proud to know that his son was ready to sacrifice his life for Imam Hussain (a.s.). Qasim went to his uncle and told him about his wishes. Imam Hussain (a.s.) lovingly looked at him and said, "Whenever I wanted to see my brother I would look at your face. How could I let you go out there and be killed? What would I answer my brother? Umme Farwa turned to Imam Hussain (a.s.) and said, "You have cared for Qasim as if he was your own son. Your brother would have wanted Qasim to sacrifice his life for you just as Ali Akbar, Aun and Muhammad have." Imam Hussain(a.s.) gave his blessings to Qasim, and helped him on to his horse.

Qasim fought the enemy as if he was an experienced soldier and not a fourteen year old boy. He killed many, one after another. When Umar Saad saw the courage of this young fighter, he ordered his troops to attack him in force. They surrounded him from all sides, and attacked him with swords, spears, daggers and arrows. An enemy soldier hit him on his head with such force that he fell from his horse. Imam Hussain (a.s.) ran to him, and found that his body had been torn to pieces. He sat near Qasim's body, and cried so much that they could hear him at his camp. "O my God what have these people done to my Qasim!" Imam Hussain (a.s.) took off his robe and wrapped the pieces of Qasim's body and rode back to the camp.

When Imam Hussain (a.s.) reached the camp, Umme Farwa came with Bibi Zainab on one side and Umme Kulthoom on the other. Imam Hussain (a.s.) looked at them and said, "My dear ladies have courage. Qasim's body may be cut to pieces but his soul is now with his father Imam Hassan (a.s.)." When he opened the robe the ladies cried a lot and Umme Farwa fainted from the shock.

Soon, all of Imam Husain's (a.s.) family were killed one by one and only Imam Hussain (a.s.) and Hazrat Abbas were left. Hazrat Abbas looked at Imam Hussain (a.s.) and said, "It is now my turn to go and fight just like the others have done. Imam Hussain (a.s.) wept and said, Abbas if you go and fight who will get water for the children." Hazrat Abbas got on his horse and went to get some water and as he passed their camp, Imam Husain's (a.s.) four year-old daughter Sakina handed him her dry water bag and said, "Please get us some water as we are very thirsty." Hazrat Abbas took the bag and put it on his shoulder. He promised Sakina that God willing he would return with water for her.

When Hazrat Abbas reached the river, the troops attacked him. He fought them so fiercely that many of them they ran away. Hazrat Abbas filled Sakina's water bag and was about to ride back towards the camp. Qays, the commander of the enemy troops ordered his troops to return and attack Hazrat Abbas. He warned them that if any water got back to Imam Hussain (a.s.), then none of them would remain alive. The troops attacked Hazrat Abbas from all sides, all this time Hazrat Abbas was more concerned about saving the water bag. During the fighting, his left arm was cut off. When the army saw that he was crippled, they surrounded him and cut off his right arm as well. Hazrat Abbas still did

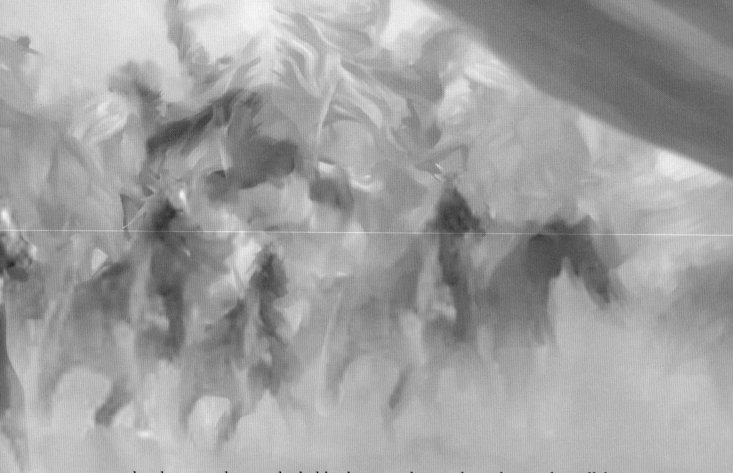

not let the water bag go, he held it between his teeth, and prayed to Allah to keep him alive long enough to reach back to thee camp and give water to his Sakina. An arrow struck the water bag and the water started gushing out. He could not get Sakina out of his mind. He kept hearing her voice again and again "O my uncle Abbas please get me some water."

The enemy continued their attack, until Hazrat Abbas finally fell from his horse. Imam Hussain (a.s.) ran towards him and put his head on his lap. Hazrat Abbas tried to open his eyes, but they were wounded and filled with blood. Hazrat Abbas said, "Thank God you have come my master. I thought I was going to die without seeing you. When I was born I saw your face first, please do not let me die without seeing it again for the last time." Imam Hussain (a.s.) wiped the blood from his eyes so that Hazrat Abbas could see him. Hazrat Abbas added, "Please do not take my body back to the camp, I do not want Sakina to see me,when I could not keep my promise to her." Imam Hussain (a.s.) said, "O Abbas I also have one request for you, I have never heard you call me brother, for once I would like to hear you call me brother." Hazrat Abbas, with his dying breath called out "My brother, my brother," Imam Hussain (a.s.) cried "O Abbas my beloved brother what have they done to you? Who is now left to fight by my side now?"

Imam Hussain (a.s.) walked back to his tent. When he got there he found Umme Rubab, with the 6 month old Ali Asgher in her arms waiting for him. She said "Our son is dying of thirst. Do something to save him." Imam Hussain (a.s.) covered Ali Asgher with his robe and took him to the battlefield. He faced the enemy and said, "O soldiers! My baby has not had any food or water for the last three days. Please have pity on him and give him a few drops of water. What crime has this innocent baby committed?" The sight of this thirsty baby in the hot sun made some of the troops cry. When Umar Saad saw this, he realised that if he did not take any action immediately then his troops might refuse to continue to fight. He ordered Hurmula to kill Ali Asgher. Hurmula put an arrow to his bow and took aim. The arrow went right through Ali Asgher's neck. Blood gushed out of his wound and splashed on to Imam Hussain (a.s.) face. Ali Asgher died in his father's arm.

Imam Hussain (a.s.) walked back to the camp weeping with Ali Asgher in his arms. At the door he waited for a moment and then turned back, this he did seven times as if he was building his strength to face the mother of the baby who had been so brutally murdered.

Umme Rubab looked at her husband's face covered in blood and cried out "What have they done to my son, did they even give him a drop of water before they killed him?" Imam Hussain (a.s.) said, "I pleaded with them to give him water, but instead they drenched him with blood." Umme Rubab said, "Please bury Ali Asgher with your own hands. After you have gone, the army of Yazid will trample over the bodies of our beloved. I want my young son spared of such treatment." Umme Rubab and the other ladies and children were all crying. Imam Hussain (a.s.) looked up and said. "O Allah bear witness that I have done my duty to the last."

Imam Hussain (a.s.) looked around him. There was no one left. He walked towards the camp weeping with all his heart, and called out. "O my dear ladies, come to me and hear my last farewell to you all. I am very sad to leave you, because I know how much you will suffer once I am gone." Everyone was crying. Imam Hussain (a.s.) turned to Bibi Zainab and said, "I am leaving the widows and orphans in your care. My dear sister please look after my Sakina especially, she has never been separated from me even for a day. Please dear sister when you get water give to her first, she hasn't asked for water since her uncle Abbas died."

"O Bibi Zainab, the enemies will take you prisoners and parade you in the streets of Kufa and Shaam. This will be a very difficult time for you. Do not give up hope, you will have to be brave." Bibi Zainab with tears rolling down her cheeks promised her brother that she would not let him down. Imam Hussain (a.s.) held his sister close to him and said, "My dear sister when you are finally free, and return to Madina give my very special salaams to my daughter Fatima Sughra. I could not bring her with me because she was sick. She will be very sad to hear about what has happened in Karbala and Shaam. Tell her that her father remembered her right to his last dying moment. Convey my salaams to my people, and tell them to remember our thirst whenever they drink water." Imam Hussain (a.s.) put his hand on Bibi Zainab's head and said goodbye to her.

Imam Hussain (a.s.) then said goodbye to the other ladies and children. He picked up his daughter Sakina, and kissed her cheeks, knowing that these same cheeks were going to be slapped by the cruel hands of Yazid's men. The look on Sakina's face as her father put her down broke his heart. Imam Hussain (a.s.) then went to his son Imam Zainul Abideen's tent. He lovingly touched his shoulder and said, "My son wake up, the time has come for me to go and face the enemy." Imam Zainul Abideen (a.s.) opened his eyes and said, "Dear father why are you alone, where is my uncle Abbas, and my brother Ali Akbar, where are my cousins and your companions." Imam Hussain (a.s.) replied that they had all died fighting bravely against the enemy. Imam Zainul Abideen (a.s.) was very sick and tried to get up so that the could join his father. Imam Hussain (a.s.) said to him, "Your duty is to be with the ladies. When they will be paraded in the streets of Kufa and Shaam, you will have to be strong and stand by your aunt Bibi Zainab."

Imam Hussain (a.s.) said farewell. He got on to his horse called Zuljanah, given by his grandfather. Zuljanah would not move forward. Imam Hussain (a.s.) looked back and saw Sakina pleading with him not to go. He got down from Zuljanah and sat on the ground holding his dear daughter, both of them crying. He explained to her that he did not want to leave her, but if he did not go, then Yazid will destroy Islam. He said, "What will I answer to my mother, when she asks me why I did not save the religion of the Prophet(saw)?" Imam Hussain (a.s.) promised Sakina that he would be with her soon.

Imam Hussain (a.s.) went to the battlefield wearing the Prophet's robe and turban. He faced the enemy and told them for the last time, "For those of you who still do not know me, I am the grandson of the Prophet, and on the right path. Yazid wants to lead you away from the truth. He does not follow the teachings of your Prophet." Umar Saad shouted to his men "do not be fooled by his words and attack him now!" Arrows were showered on Imam Hussain (a.s.). He charged into the battlefield like a lion, saying, "If you are determined to fight me then I am ready, watch how the grandson of the Prophet (s.a.w.) fights, see how the son of Ali and Fatima fights. Even after three days of hunger and thirst, I am not afraid to die. For me death is better than surrender."

When the enemy saw Imam Hussain (a.s.) charging towards them, they thought for a moment that Imam Ali (a.s.) had come down from the heavens to take revenge on them. Many of them ran away. When Umar Saad saw the fear on their faces, he sent his bravest soldiers to fight Imam Hussain (a.s.). There was not a single member in Yazid's army who could stand in front of Imam Hussain (a.s.). The enemy troops surrounded him from all sides, but he defeated them all. Umar Saad stood back and watched, amazed at how Imam Hussain (a.s.) who had suffered so much, was still fighting so bravely.

While Imam Hussain (a.s.) continued fighting Angel Jibraeel came down from the heavens and said, "O My Imam! Allah is indeed pleased with your bravery. The moment has now come for you to save Islam." Imam Hussain (a.s.) returned his sword back into the sheath so that he could prepare for Asr prayers. He did not delay his prayers even while he was in the middle of a war. When Umar Saad saw this he ordered his army to attack him in force. Some of them threw stones, while some attacked him with swords and others with arrows. Imam Hussain (a.s.) was very badly wounded, he was bleeding from head to toe.

Zuljanah stopped, and Imam Hussain (a.s.) fell, his body resting on the sharp blades of the arrows. Imam Hussain (a.s.) hit his hands on the burning sands of Karbala so that he may do his tayammum, and begin his Asr prayers. Umar Saad ordered Shimr to behead Imam Hussain (a.s.). Shimr without any hesitation beheaded our Imam. The earth trembled. The sky went red with rage. The sun went into eclipse. The whole earth was crying!

Bibi Zainab ran to Imam Zainul Abideen (a.s.) and told him what had just happened. They stood silently, tears rolling down their cheeks. A strong gust of wind blew on the desert. They felt as if nature itself was crying with them. The silence was only broken by the beating of drums from the enemy camp. They were celebrating their victory. It was indeed a hollow victory, won by a well fed huge army fighting against an army of 72 brave warriors, who died hungry and thirsty.

AFTER KARBALA

That evening the enemy soldiers rushed into Imam Husain's (a.s.) camp and looted everything in sight. One of the men pulled Sakina's earrings off, ripping her ear lobes. Sakina ran out of the tent crying, her ears bleeding. Outside she met a kind old man. He wiped the blood from her ears. When Sakina saw how kind he was she asked him if he would show her the way to Najaf where her grandfather was buried. She told him that she was going to complain to him about how they killed her father and didn't let her uncle Abbas bring any water for her. When the old man saw how upset Bibi Sakina was, he comforted her and then took her back to her Aunty Bibi Zainab. The troops snatched the veils off the ladies heads, and then set fire to their tents. Bibi Zainab was very distressed. She turned to Imam Zainul Abideen (a.s.) and said, "You are our Imam now. Tell us what we should do now, should we stay in our tents and burn, or go out without

our veils ?" Imam Zainul Abideen (a.s.) told her that it was their religious duty to try and save their lives. Bibi Zainab gathered everyone and waited outside, while their homes burnt down. When the fire was out, they took shelter under one of the tents which had not been completely destroyed.

That night Umar Saad sent some bread and water to Imam Hussain's (a.s.) camp. When Bibi Zainab saw the bread and water she cried. "Imam Hussain (a.s.) and his brave soldiers had died hungry and thirsty, and now the same people who killed them were bringing bread and water to their widows and orphans." She looked at the sky and prayed to Allah to give her courage. Bibi Zainab remembered the words of her brother to give water to Sakina. When Sakina heard that there was some water, she said, "Has my uncle Abbas come back? Dear aunt, please give some water to my brother Ali Asgher first, as he is the youngest." Sakina then started to cry, she remembered what had happened that day. There was no uncle Abbas to bring her water and there was no little Asgher to play with. There was only sadness.

The next morning Umar Saad ordered that all the remaining members of Imam Husain's family were to be taken as prisoners to Kufa. Imam Zainul Abideen (a.s.) pleaded with them to allow him to bury their martyrs, but the guards refused. They were made to wait in the hot sun while the enemy spent the rest of the day burying their own dead.

The prisoners were chained around their necks, hands and feet, and put on bare camel backs. Imam Zainul Abideen (a.s.) was made to walk barefoot on the hot desert sand, even though he was sick. At the front of the caravan the guards carried spears with the heads of our Imam and his loved ones mounted on them. The guards beat the prisoners, if they complained of anything. They did not even spare they youngest. Some children died along the way, and their bodies were left in the desert. By the time they reached Kufa they were bruised all over the bodies.

Ibn Ziyad, the governor of Kufa ordered the streets to be decorated. When the caravan reached the city the people were jeering and making fun of the prisoners. But when some of the people saw the head of Imam Hussain (a.s.) on the spear they turned their heads and started to cry. They felt guilty that they allowed this

to happen to Imam Hussain (a.s.) when this same Imam was ready to help them when they needed him. It was noon and the sun was blazing hot. The children were crying of hunger and thirst. As the caravan reached the governor's palace, Bibi Zainab faced the crowd and said, "Do you know who your governor has killed? We are the grand children of your Prophet (s.a.w.). When your governor killed the Prophet's loved ones, the skies cried and the earth shook. Where were you then? There was complete silence in the crowd. Some people realised their mistake and started to cry with shame. When Umar Saad saw what was happening he quickly led the prisoners into the palace.

When Ibn Ziyad saw Imam Zainul Abideen (a.s.) in the palace he ordered him to be killed straight away. Bibi Zainab ran in front of him and said, "You will have to kill me first. How dare you sit on this throne which does not rightfully

belong to you and insult us. Listen, O son of Ziyad we are the grand children of the Prophet. You should be ashamed of yourself. You claim to follow the Prophet's teachings, yet you have done everything to destroy his family." Ibn Ziyad was surprised at how brave this lady was. He thought that after all that they had suffered, they would not have the strength to face him. More and more people started to realize that what Bibi Zainab was saying was true. Ibn Ziyad ordered the prisoner to be taken to the prison next to the palace immediately. He told Shimr and Khooli to make preparations to take the prisoners to Shaam (Damascus) before they had a chance to speak out in public again.

As the caravan was leaving Kufa, people watched from the rooftops. Bibi Zainab and other prisoners continued to tell the people about what had happened in Karbala. Many people started speaking out against Ibn Ziyad. On the journey the prisoners again suffered in the hands of the guards. When the caravan

reached Shaam, the prisoners had to wait in the hot sun while Shimr went to Yazid's palace to announce their arrival. Yazid had declared that day as a day of celebration. Every corner of the city was decorated.

The prisoners were finally taken to Yazid's palace. Yazid looked at little Sakina and said that he was going to have this little girl as his slave. Bibi Zainab was furious, she shouted "O Yazid have you lost your sense of shame? You want to make the grand children of the Prophet (s.a.w.) your slave?" Yazid shouted at Bibi Zainab "I am the truthful one, Allah is pleased with my victory. He has humiliated your family and caused the death of your brother Hussain." Bibi Zainab was very angry at Yazid. She could not just stand there while this wicked and corrupt man spoke like this. She said, "Do you think that it was Allah who made you commit these awful crimes? Do you blame Allah for the sufferings that you have caused us? Do you blame Allah for the death of the grandson of the Prophet (s.a.w.)? No, Yazid, it was you who caused all these sufferings. Did you think that by killing the grandson of the Prophet you have won the battle? No Yazid you haven't. It is my brother Imam Hussain (a.s.) who by sacrificing his life in Karbala has made sure that evil men like you would not be allowed to destroy Islam. The victory is not yours. The victory is of Imam Hussain (a.s.). The victory is surely of Islam !"

Yazid was amazed at how this lady after all that she had gone through could talk to him like this. He then thought that Imam Zainul Abideen (a.s.) would be an easier target for his insults, as he looked too sick to be able to answer him back. He turned to Imam Zainul Abideen (a.s.) and said, "Well, who do you think the winner of this war is?" Imam Zainul Abideen (a.s.) replied, "Yazid, victory can only belong to those who are on the right path. Look at you, and then look at my father Imam Hussain (a.s.). My father, who was killed so brutally by your order was the grandson of the Prophet (s.a.w.). Yazid, you are the grandson of Abu Sufyan, the enemy of the Prophet (s.a.w.) and Islam just as you are."

Yazid, to stop Imam Zainul Abideen (a.s.) from saying anything further, ordered the Adhaan to be given, as if to prove his faith. When the reciter called out "Ash-ha-du anna Muhammadan Rasulullah", Imam Zainul Abideen (a.s.) turned to Yazid and said, "O Yazid just listen! The Messenger of Allah who is mentioned in the Adhaan, is he your grandfather or ours?" Yazid was so angry that he ordered the prisoners to be taken away immediately and put into the prison. As soon as the prison doors were closed they started saying their prayers to thank Allah (s.w.t.). In the prison it was so dark that you could not tell whether it was day or night. The days were so hot that it was difficult to breath and the nights were so cold that Sakina's toes would turn blues. They had nothing to sleep on but the bare floor.

One night Sakina suddenly started to cry in her sleep. When her mother asked her what the matter was she said that she saw her father in her dreams. Everyone started to cry so much that the noise reached Yazid at the palace. He asked the guards what all the noise was about. When they told him what it was, he ordered that Imam Hussain's (a.s.) head be taken to Sakina in order to keep her quiet. The guards brought the head, and put it on the ground.

When Sakina saw her father's head, she hugged it. All the ladies were stricken with grief. Sakina complained to her father about how the evil men snatched her earrings that he had given to her, how they took away their veils, and burnt their tents. Suddenly Sakina stopped complaining and was completely quiet. Inna Lillahi Wa Inna Ilayhi Raaji'oon. Sakina, the loving daughter of Imam Hussain (a.s.) passed away. Imam Zainul Abideen (a.s.) buried her in a small grave in the small corner of the prison. All the ladies sat by Sakina's mother Rubab and cried. Sakina will finally be able to sleep on her father's chest once again.

After the death of Sakina, the people of Shaam started to question Yazid about the prisoners. Many felt that they had already spent so long in prison in the worst possible condition. What crime had they committed to deserve such harsh treatment. Yazid realized that if he did not do anything to change the situation, the people will turn against him. He made arrangements for the prisoners to be brought to the palace court to be set free. Many people were invited to see the event. When everybody was seated, an announcement was made that the great grandson of the Prophet was entering the court. The ladies of his household were seated behind the curtain which was put up especially for the occasion.

When Imam Zainul Abideen (a.s.) walked in everyone stood up. They could not believe what they saw. Even though the chains had been removed, Imam Zainul Abideen (a.s.) could hardly walk. His neck, hands and feet were deeply cut and bleeding and his back bent because of the way he was chained. There was, dignity in his face, never at any time had he bowed down to Yazid. Yazid told Imam Zainul Abideen (a.s.) that they were free to leave, and offered them any amount that they were required. Bibi Zainab said from behind the curtain "O Yazid, haven't you done enough to us? You still want to insult us by this offer. Your actions can only be judged by Allah (s.w.t.). You will have to answer

to Him and the Prophet for all that you have done. All that we want are the heads of our martyrs and our property which your men looted from us. They took away the veil given to me by my mother, they took away the bloodstained clothes of my brother, Sakina's earrings given to her by her father. No there is nothing you can give us to replace these things, which mean more to us than anything else". Yazid was amazed at her answer. He promised to give back everything that was taken from them in Karbala.

Imam Zainul Abideen (a.s.) and the rest of the ladies and children stayed in Shaam for a few more days and then made preparations to travel to Karbala, to pay their respects to their martyrs, and then go back to Madina. They went back to the prison to say goodbye to Sakina. Sakina's mother Rubab fell on the grave crying, "O my dear Sakina, we are finally free to go home. But my child you are still imprisoned in Shaam. What will I tell your sister Fatima Sughra, when she asks about you. My Sakina I am leaving but my heart and soul will always be here with you. O people of Shaam, look after the grave of my child Sakina."

Finally, the grand children of the Prophet (s.a.w.) left Shaam. Imam Zainul Abideen (a.s.) led the caravan towards Karbala. Everyone was very quiet. They were all thinking about their loved ones. When they arrived in Karbala, they sat by the graves, crying and remembering that tragic day on the tenth of Muharram when they lost so many of their loved ones. Finally, after saying goodbye to their martyrs they started the journey back to Madina. How sad this journey must have been. Even though they were now free, their hearts were in Karbala and Shaam.

When the caravan reached Madina, Fatima Sughra ran to her aunt Bibi Zainab and her brother Imam Zainul Abideen (a.s.) and asked them about her sister Sakina. When they told her that she had died in the prison in Shaam she screamed, "O my God, if my Sakina was not there, then who played with my little brother Ali Asghar?" Imam Zainul Abideen (a.s.) held her close and said,

"My dear sister, those evil men did not even leave our innocent little brother. When his throat was dry from thirst, instead of giving him some water they shot an arrow right through his throat. O my sister, how can I explain to you the pain and grief that our father had to go through when he carried the body of his young son Ali Akbar." Fatima Sughra could not take it any more. She fainted into the hands of her brother. Everyone around them was crying, such sorrow had never before been seen in Madina.

Bibi Zainab (a.s.) visited the grave of her grandfather, the Prophet (s.a.w.). She sat by his grave and complained, with tears in her eyes. "O my grandfather look at what Yazid and his men did to your grandchildren. They killed your most beloved grandson, Imam Hussain (a.s.). They killed Abbas, when he went to get water for Sakina. They killed Ali Akbar, who looked like you.

They killed my brother's son Qasim. They killed my sons Aun and Muhammad. They didn't even leave little Asgher. O my dear grandfather, your beloved Sakina is also gone. She died in the dark prison of Shaam." Bibi Zainab then went to the grave of her mother Fatima (a.s.) and cried, "O my dear mother, look at how they treated us? See these bloodstained clothes of your son. O my mother, they paraded us in the streets of Kufa and Shaam without our veils." A voice came from the grave, "My dear child I saw what they did. I was there when they beheaded my Hussain. I was there when the guards slapped Sakina just for crying for her dead father. I was there when they paraded you on the streets without your veils." Bibi Zainab cried "O my dear mother, I have so much to tell you."

فَاَسْأَلُ اللهَ الَّذي أَكْرَمَني بِمَعْرِفَتِكُمْ وَمَعْرِفَةِ اَوْلِيائِكُمْ وَرَزَقَني الْبَراءَةَ مِنْ اَعْدائِكُمْ

اَنْ يَجْعَلَني مَعَكُمْ في الدُّنْيا وَالآخِرَةِ وَاَنْ يُثَبِّتَ لي عِنْدَكُمْ قَدَمَ صِدْقٍ في الدُّنْيا وَالآخِرَةِ

وَاَسْأَلُهُ اَنْ يُبَلِّغَني الْمَقامَ الْمَحْمُودَ لَكُمْ عِنْدَ اللهِ وَاَنْ يَرْزُقَني طَلَبَ ثاري مَعَ اِمامٍ هُدىً ظاهِرٍ ناطِقٍ بِالْحَقِّ مِنْكُ

وَاَسْأَلُ اللهَ بِحَقِّكُمْ وَبِالشَّأْنِ الَّذي لَكُمْ عِنْدَهُ اَنْ يُعْطِيَني بِمُصابي بِكُمْ اَفْضَلَ ما يُعْطي مُصاباً بِمُصيبَتِهِ

مُصيبَةً ما اَعْظَمَها وَاَعْظَمَ رَزِيَّتَها في الْاِسْلامِ وَفي جَميعِ السَّماواتِ وَالْاَرْضِ

اَللّـهُمَّ اجْعَلْني في مَقامي هذا مِمَّنْ تَنالُهُ مِنْكَ صَلَواتٌ وَرَحْمَةٌ وَمَغْفِرَةٌ، اَللّـهُمَّ اجْعَلْ مَحْياىَ مَحْيا مُحَمَّدٍ وَآلِ مُحَمَّ

وَمَماتي مَماتَ مُحَمَّدٍ وَآلِ مُحَمَّدٍ، اَللّـهُمَّ اِنَّ هذا يَوْمٌ تَبَرَّكَتْ بِهِ بَنُو اُمَيَّةَ وَابْنُ آكِلَةِ الْاَكْبادِ اللَّعينُ ابْنُ اللَّعينِ

عَلى لِسانِكَ وَلِسانِ نَبِيِّكَ صَلَّى اللهُ عَلَيْهِ وَآلِهِ في كُلِّ مَوْطِنٍ وَمَوْقِفٍ وَقَفَ فيهِ نَبِيُّكَ صَلَّى اللهُ عَلَيْهِ وَآلِهِ،

اَللّـهُمَّ الْعَنْ اَبا سُفْيانَ وَمُعاوِيَةَ وَيَزيدَ ابْنَ مُعاوِيَةَ عَلَيْهِمْ مِنْكَ اللَّعْنَةُ اَبَدَ الْآبِدينَ، وَهذا يَوْمٌ فَرِحَتْ بِهِ

آلُ زِيادٍ وَآلُ مَرْوانَ بِقَتْلِهِمُ الْحُسَيْنَ صَلَواتُ اللهِ عَلَيْهِ، اَللّـهُمَّ فَضاعِفْ عَلَيْهِمُ اللَّعْنَ مِنْكَ وَالْعَذابَ (الْاَليمَ)

اَللّـهُمَّ اِنّي اَتَقَرَّبُ اِلَيْكَ في هذا الْيَوْمِ وَفي مَوْقِفي هذا وَاَيّامِ حَياتي بِالْبَراءَةِ مِنْهُمْ وَاللَّعْنَةِ عَلَيْهِمْ

وَبِالْمُوالاةِ لِنَبِيِّكَ وَآلِ نَبِيِّكَ عَلَيْهِ وَعَلَيْهِمُ السَّلامُ

ثُمَّ تَقول مائة مرّة: اَللّـهُمَّ الْعَنْ اَوَّلَ ظالِمٍ ظَلَمَ حَقَّ مُحَمَّدٍ وَآلِ مُحَمَّدٍ وَآخِرَ تابِعٍ لَهُ عَلى ذلِكَ،

اَللّـهُمَّ الْعَنِ الْعِصابَةَ الَّتي جاهَدَتِ الْحُسَيْنَ عَلَيْهِ السَّلامُ وَشايَعَتْ وَبايَعَتْ وَتابَعَتْ عَلى قَتْلِهِ اَللّـهُمَّ الْعَنْهُمْ جَميعاً

ثُمَّ تَقول مائة مرّة: اَلسَّلامُ عَلَيْكَ يا اَبا عَبْدِاللهِ وَعَلَى الْاَرْواحِ الَّتي حَلَّتْ بِفِنائِكَ عَلَيْكَ مِنّي سَلامُ اللهِ اَبَداً ما بَقيتُ وَبَقِيَ

اللَّيْلُ وَالنَّهارُ عَلَيْكَ مِنّي سَلامُ اللهِ اَبَداً ما بَقيتُ وَبَقِيَ اللَّيْلُ وَالنَّهارُ وَلا جَعَلَهُ اللهُ آخِرَ الْعَهْدِ مِنّي لِزِيارَتِكُمْ، وَلا جَعَلَهُ اللهُ

آخِرَ الْعَهْدِ مِنّي لِزِيارَتِكُمْ، اَلسَّلامُ عَلَى الْحُسَيْنِ وَعَلى عَلِيِّ بْنِ الْحُسَيْنِ وَعَلى اَوْلادِ الْحُسَيْنِ وَعَلى اَصْحابِ الْحُسَيْنِ،

ثُمَّ تَقول : اَللّـهُمَّ خُصَّ اَنْتَ اَوَّلَ ظالِمٍ بِاللَّعْنِ مِنّي وَابْدَأْ بِهِ اَوَّلاً ثُمَّ (الْعَنِ) الثّانِيَ وَالثّالِثَ وَالرّابِعَ اَللّـهُمَّ الْعَنْ يَزيدَ خامِساً

اَللّـهُمَّ الْعَنْ يَزيدَ خامِساً وَالْعَنْ عُبَيْدَ اللهِ بْنَ زِيادٍ وَابْنَ مَرْجانَةَ وَعُمَرَ بْنَ سَعْدٍ وَشِمْراً وَآلَ اَبي سُفْيانَ وَآلَ زِيادٍ

وَآلَ مَرْوانَ اِلى يَوْمِ الْقِيامَةِ ثُمَّ تسجد وتقول: اَللّـهُمَّ لَكَ الْحَمْدُ حَمْدَ الشّاكِرينَ لَكَ عَلى مُصابِهِمُ الْحَمْدُ للهِ عَلى عَظيمِ رَزِيَّتي

اَللّـهُمَّ ارْزُقْني شَفاعَةَ الْحُسَيْنِ يَوْمَ الْوُرُودِ وَثَبِّتْ لي قَدَمَ صِدْقٍ عِنْدَكَ مَعَ الْحُسَيْنِ وَاَصْحابِ الْحُسَيْنِ

اَلَّذينَ بَذَلُوا مُهَجَهُمْ دُونَ الْحُسَيْنِ عَلَيْهِ السَّلامُ .

ZIYARAT ASHURA

اَلسَّلامُ عَلَيْكَ يا اَبا عَبْدِاللهِ، اَلسَّلامُ عَلَيْكَ يَا بْنَ رَسُولِ اللهِ اَلسَّلامُ عَلَيْكَ يا خِيَرَةَ اللهِ وابْنَ خِيَرَتِهِ

اَلسَّلامُ عَلَيْكَ يَا بْنَ اَمِيرِ الْمُؤْمِنينَ وابْنَ سَيِّدِ الْوَصِيِّينَ، اَلسَّلامُ عَلَيْكَ يَا بْنَ فاطِمَةَ سَيِّدَةِ نِساءِ الْعالَمينَ،

اَلسَّلامُ عَلَيْكَ يا ثارَ اللهِ وابْنَ ثارِهِ وَالْوِتْرَ الْمَوْتُورَ، اَلسَّلامُ عَلَيْكَ وَعَلَى الأَرْواحِ الَّتي حَلَّتْ بِفِنائِكَ

عَلَيْكُمْ مِنّي جَميعاً سَلامُ اللهِ اَبَداً ما بَقيتُ وَبَقِيَ اللَّيْلُ وَالنَّهارُ، يا اَبا عَبْدِاللهِ لَقَدْ عَظُمَتِ الرَّزِيَّةُ

وَجَلَّتْ وَعَظُمَتِ الْمُصيبَةُ بِكَ عَلَيْنا وَعَلَى جَميعِ اَهْلِ الأِسْلامِ

وَجَلَّتْ وَعَظُمَتْ مُصيبَتُكَ فِي السَّماواتِ عَلى جَميعِ اَهْلِ السَّماواتِ،

فَلَعَنَ اللهُ اُمَّةً اَسَّسَتْ اَساسَ الظُّلْمِ وَالْجَوْرِ عَلَيْكُمْ اَهْلَ الْبَيْتِ،

وَلَعَنَ اللهُ اُمَّةً دَفَعَتْكُمْ عَنْ مَقامِكُمْ وَاَزالَتْكُمْ عَنْ مَراتِبِكُمُ الَّتي رَتَّبَكُمُ اللهُ فيها، وَلَعَنَ اللهُ اُمَّةً قَتَلَتْكُمْ

وَلَعَنَ اللهُ الْمُمَهِّدينَ لَهُمْ بِالتَّمْكينِ مِنْ قِتالِكُمْ، بَرِئْتُ اِلَى اللهِ وَاِلَيْكُمْ مِنْهُمْ وَمِنْ اَشْياعِهِمْ وَاَتْباعِهِمْ وَاَوْلِيائِهِمْ،

يا اَبا عَبْدِاللهِ اِنّي سِلْمٌ لِمَنْ سالَمَكُمْ وَحَرْبٌ لِمَنْ حارَبَكُمْ اِلَى يَوْمِ الْقِيامَةِ، وَلَعَنَ اللهُ آلَ زِيادٍ وَآلَ مَرْوانَ،

وَلَعَنَ اللهُ بَني اُمَيَّةَ قاطِبَةً، وَلَعَنَ اللهُ ابْنَ مَرْجانَةَ وَلَعَنَ اللهُ عُمَرَ بْنَ سَعْدٍ، وَلَعَنَ اللهُ شِمْراً،

وَلَعَنَ اللهُ اُمَّةً اَسْرَجَتْ وَاَلْجَمَتْ وَتَنَقَّبَتْ لِقِتالِكَ، بِاَبي اَنْتَ وَاُمّي لَقَدْ عَظُمَ مُصابي بِكَ

فَاَسْاَلُ اللهَ الَّذي اَكْرَمَ مَقامَكَ وَاَكْرَمَني بِكَ اَنْ يَرْزُقَني طَلَبَ ثارِكَ مَعَ اِمامٍ مَنْصُورٍ مِنْ اَهْلِ بَيْتِ مُحَمَّدٍ صَلَّى اللهُ عَلَيْهِ وَآلِهِ،

اَنْ يَرْزُقَني طَلَبَ ثارِكَ مَعَ اِمامٍ مَنْصُورٍ مِنْ اَهْلِ بَيْتِ مُحَمَّدٍ صَلَّى اللهُ عَلَيْهِ وَآلِهِ،

اَللّـهُمَّ اجْعَلْني عِنْدَكَ وَجيهاً بِالْحُسَيْنِ عَلَيْهِ السَّلامُ فِي الدُّنْيا وَالأخِرَةِ، يا اَبا عَبْدِاللهِ اِنّي اَتَقَرَّبُ اِلَى اللهِ

وَ اِلى رَسُولِهِ وَاِلى اَميرِ الْمُؤْمِنينَ وَاِلى فاطِمَةَ وَاِلَى الْحَسَنِ وَاِلَيْكَ بِمُوالاتِكَ

وَبِالْبَراءَةِ مِمَّنْ قاتَلَكَ وَنَصَبَ لَكَ الْحَرْبَ وَبِالْبَراءَةِ مِمَّنْ اَسَّسَ اَساسَ الظُّلْمِ وَالْجَوْرِ عَلَيْكُمْ

وَاَبْرَأُ اِلَى اللهِ وَاِلى رَسُولِهِ مِمَّنْ اَسَّسَ اَساسَ ذلِكَ وَبَنى عَلَيْهِ بُنْيانَهُ

وَجَرى في ظُلْمِهِ وَجَوْرِهِ عَلَيْكُمْ وَعَلى اَشْياعِكُمْ، بَرِئْتُ اِلَى اللهِ وَاِلَيْكُمْ مِنْهُمْ

وَاَتَقَرَّبُ اِلَى اللهِ ثُمَّ اِلَيْكُمْ بِمُوالاتِكُمْ وَمُوالاةِ وَلِيِّكُمْ وَبِالْبَراءَةِ مِنْ اَعْدائِكُمْ وَالنّاصِبينَ لَكُمُ الْحَرْبَ

وَبِالْبَراءَةِ مِنْ اَشْياعِهِمْ وَاَتْباعِهِمْ، اِنّي سِلْمٌ لِمَنْ سالَمَكُمْ وَحَرْبٌ لِمَنْ حارَبَكُمْ وَوَلِيٌّ لِمَنْ والاكُمْ وَعَدُوٌّ لِمَنْ عاداكُمْ

Peace be upon you O' Aba 'Abdillah; Peace be upon you O' son of the Messenger of Allah; Peace be upon you O' son of the Commander of the Faithful and the son of the leader of the inheritors (of the Prophet); Peace be upon you O' son of Fatimah, the leader of the women of the entire Universe.

Peace be upon you O' the one who was killed and whose blood has not yet been avenged – and whose avenging is in the hands of Allah and peace be upon you, the son of one who was killed and whose blood has not yet been avenged (Imam 'Ali b. Abi Talib) and peace be upon you O' the one who was alone, an individual (killed). Peace be upon you and also upon those souls who accompanied you to your annihilation.

Upon you and upon all of those (who were killed) is the Salam of Allah from me for eternity, as long as the night and the day remain.

O' Aba 'Abdillah! Surely the tribulations are great and unbearable and your tragedy is great for us, and for all the people of Islam and unbearable and great is your tragedy in the heavens and for all of the dwellers of the heavens.

May the curse (La'n) be upon those people who laid down the foundations for the oppression and wrongs done upon you, the family of the Prophet [Ahlul Bayt].

May Allah curse those people who denied you your position (O' Ahlul Bayt) and removed you from your rank which Allah himself had granted you

May the curse of Allah be upon those people who killed you and may the curse of Allah be upon those people who made it easy for them by preparing the grounds of your killing.

I turn to Allah and I turn towards you and turn away from them and their adherents, followers and friends.

O' Aba 'Abdillah! I am at peace with those who make peace with you and I am at war with those who make war with you until the Day of Judgment.

May the curse of Allah be upon the family of Ziyad and the family of Marwan and may the curse of Allah be upon Bani Umayyah.

And may the curse of Allah be upon the nation that carried out, saw and were silent at your killing.

May my father and mother be sacrificed for you. Surely my sorrow for you is great and I pray to Allah who has honored your status and has also honoured me through you that He grant me the opportunity to seek your revenge with the victorious Imam from the family of Muhammad.

O' Allah! Make me worthy of respect with You through Husayn, peace be upon him, both in the transient world and also the next life.

O' Aba 'Abdillah! Surely I seek closeness to Allah and to His Messenger and to the Commander of the Faithful and to Fatimah and to Hasan and to you through love of you and through distancing myself from those who laid the foundations and those who built upon and carried out oppression and cruelty upon you all and upon your followers.

I disassociate myself from them through Allah and through all of you and I seek nearness to Allah and then to you through love for you and your friends and disassociation with your enemies and from those who want to fight against you and disassociation from their adherents and followers.

Surely I am at peace with those who are at peace with you and I am at war with those who are at war with you and I am a friends to those who are friends to you and I am an enemy to those who are enemies to you.

So then I ask Allah who has honoured me with a cognizance of all of you and a cognizance of your friends that He also grant me the opportunity to disassociate myself from your enemies and that He place me with you – both in the transient world and also in the next life – and that he make me firm in your presence with a truthful stance both in the transient world and also the next life.

And I ask Him (Allah) that He enables me to reach to the honoured station with you in the presence of Allah and that He grant me the ability to seek the revenge of you with the rightly guided Imam from you, who shall surely come and speak the truth.

And I ask Allah for your sake and for the status and rank which you have with Him that He grant me that thing due to me showing grief and sorrow at your sorrows even more than of that which he gives in a person's own grief and sorrows, and what great sorrow and tragedies you faced! How great was your tragedy for Islam and for all of the inhabitants of the heavens and the Earth!

O' Allah! Make me at this moment, one who receives from You prayers, mercy and forgiveness.

O' Allah! Make me live the life of Muhammad and the family of Muhammad and permit me to die the death of Muhammad and the family of Muhammad.

O' Allah! This is the day (the Day of 'Ashura) which the Bani Umayyah rejoiced upon (and is the day when the) son of the liver eater (the son of Hind b. Abu Sufyan – Mu'awiyah and his son Yazid) celebrated, the cursed son(s) (Yazid) of the cursed (Mu'awiyah), as said by You and Your Prophet at every place and occasion.

O' Allah! Curse Abu Sufyan and Mu'awiyah and Yazid b. Mu'awiyah – upon them may Your curse be forever and eternity. And this is the day when the family of Ziyad were happy and so were the family of Marwan at their killing of Husayn, may the Prayers of Allah be upon him. O' Allah! Increase upon them Your curse and (Your) painful punishment.

O' Allah! Surely I seek nearness to you on this day (the Day of 'Ashura) and in this place (which I am in) and in all days of my life by disassociating myself from these people and sending curses upon them and through my love and friendship to Your Prophet and the family of Your Prophet, peace be upon him and upon all of them.

O' Allah! Curse the first tyrant who oppressed the right of Muhammad and the family of Muhammad and the next person who followed him on this path. O' Allah! Curse the group who fought against Husayn and those who followed them and supported them and assisted them in killing him. O' Allah, curse all of them!

Peace be upon you O' Aba 'Abdillah and upon the souls which were annihilated with you. Upon you, from me, is the peace of Allah for eternity, as long as the night and the day remain and please do not make this (Ziyarat) as my last contact with you. Greetings be upon Husayn, and upon 'Ali the son of Husayn and upon the children of Husayn and upon the companions of Husayn.

O' Allah! Particularly curse the first tyrant, a curse from me, and begin the first curse with him and then send the curse on the second and the third and then the forth (tyrant). O' Allah curse Yazid, the fifth (tyrant) and curse 'Ubaydullah b. Ziyad and Ibne Marjanah and 'Umar b. Sa'd and Shimr and the family of Sufyan and the family of Ziyad and the family of Marwan until the day of Judgement.

O' Allah! To you belongs the praise, the praise of those who are thankful to You for their tribulations. All Praise belongs to Allah for my intense grief. O' Allah, grant me the blessing of intercession of Husayn on the Day of Appearance (before You) and strengthen me with a truthful stand in Your presence along with Husayn and the companions of Husayn – those people who sacrificed everything for Husayn, peace be upon him.